W9-AKD-572

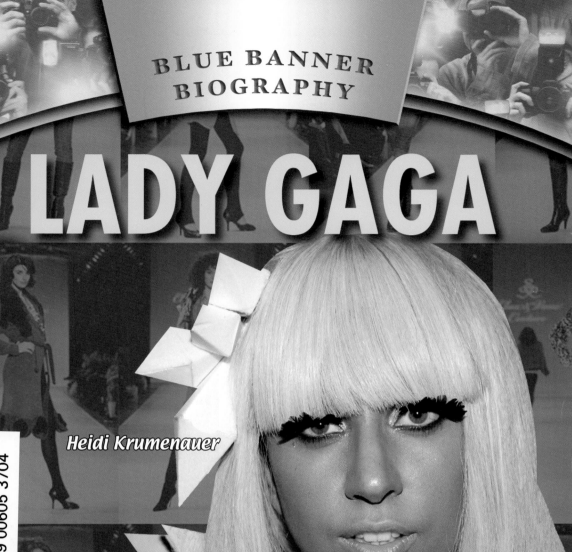

BLUE BANNER BIOGRAPHY

LADY GAGA

Heidi Krumenauer

Mitchell Lane
PUBLISHERS

P.O. Box 196
Hockessin, Delaware 19707
Visit us on the web: www.mitchelllane.com
Comments? email us: mitchelllane@mitchelllane.com

Mitchell Lane

Printing   1   2   3   4   5   6   7   8   9

Blue Banner Biographies

Akon	Flo Rida	Megan Fox
Alicia Keys	Gwen Stefani	Miguel Tejada
Allen Iverson	Ice Cube	Missy Elliott
Ashanti	Ja Rule	Nancy Pelosi
Ashlee Simpson	Jamie Foxx	Natasha Bedingfield
Ashton Kutcher	Jay-Z	Orianthi
Avril Lavigne	Jennifer Lopez	Orlando Bloom
Beyoncé	Jessica Simpson	P. Diddy
Blake Lively	J. K. Rowling	Peyton Manning
Bow Wow	Joe Flacco	Pink
Brett Favre	John Legend	Queen Latifah
Britney Spears	Johnny Depp	Rihanna
Carrie Underwood	Justin Berfield	Robert Pattinson
Chris Brown	Justin Timberlake	Ron Howard
Chris Daughtry	Kanye West	Sean Kingston
Christina Aguilera	Kate Hudson	Selena
Christopher Paul Curtis	Keith Urban	Shakira
Ciara	Kelly Clarkson	Shia LaBeouf
Clay Aiken	Kenny Chesney	Shontelle Layne
Cole Hamels	Kristen Stewart	Soulja Boy Tell 'Em
Condoleezza Rice	**Lady Gaga**	Stephenie Meyer
Corbin Bleu	Lance Armstrong	Taylor Swift
Daniel Radcliffe	Leona Lewis	T.I.
David Ortiz	Lil Wayne	Timbaland
David Wright	Lindsay Lohan	Tim McGraw
Derek Jeter	Mariah Carey	Toby Keith
Drew Brees	Mario	Usher
Eminem	Mary J. Blige	Vanessa Anne Hudgens
Eve	Mary-Kate and Ashley Olsen	Zac Efron
Fergie		

Library of Congress Cataloging-in-Publication Data
Krumenauer, Heidi.
  Lady Gaga / by Heidi Krumenauer.
    p. cm. — (Blue banner biographies)
  Includes bibliographical references, discography, and index.
  ISBN 978-1-58415-904-9 (library bound)
  1. Lady Gaga—Juvenile literature. 2. Singers—United States—
Biography—Juvenile literature. I. Title.
  ML3930.L13.K78 2011
  782.42164092—dc22
  [B]
                                    2010008944

PARENTS AND TEACHERS STRONGLY CAUTIONED: The story of Lady Gaga's life may not be appropriate for younger readers.

ABOUT THE AUTHOR: Heidi Krumenauer has written more than 1,200 newspaper and magazine articles. Since 2006, she has contributed chapters to nearly a dozen nonfiction book projects. She is a regular contributor to several print and online publications. Heidi's first book—*Why Does Grandma Have a Wibble?*—was released in 2007. She is also the author of *Brett Favre*, *Rihanna*, *Jimmie Johnson*, *Joe Flacco*, *Sean Kingston*, and *Flo Rida* for Mitchell Lane Publishers. Heidi graduated from the University of Wisconsin—Platteville with a degree in Technical Communications Management. She is in upper management for a Fortune 400 insurance company. Heidi and her husband, Jeff, raise their two sons, Noah and Payton, in Southern Wisconsin.

PUBLISHER'S NOTE: The following story has been thoroughly researched, and to the best of our knowledge represents a true story. While every possible effort has been made to ensure accuracy, the publisher will not assume liability for damages caused by inaccuracies in the data and makes no warranty on the accuracy of the information contained herein. This story has not been authorized or endorsed by Lady Gaga.

Blue Banner Biography

Lady Gaga was the life of the party with her fireworks bra at the MuchMusic Awards on June 21, 2009. Gaga took home an award for Best International Video by an Artist.

Knowing When to Be a Lady

It doesn't seem to happen very often, but Lady Gaga has, on occasion, ditched her wacky masks and trendy attire to take on a serious role when in the presence of royalty and world leaders. On October 10, 2009, she shared the stage with the President of the United States, where she sang from a white grand piano at the Human Rights Campaign dinner in Washington, D.C., wearing a little black dress and dark sunglasses with round lenses. President Barack Obama told the audience, "It's a privilege to open tonight for Lady Gaga. I've made it." Lady Gaga acknowledged the President by standing to applause.

Two months later, on December 7, 2009, the reigning queen of pop met the reigning queen of England, Elizabeth II. At the Queen's Royal Variety Performance, the annual benefit for England's Entertainment Artistes' Benevolent Fund in Blackpool, England, Lady Gaga performed "Speechless," a song she wrote for her father. She wore a full-length red latex dress with a 20-foot cloak, Elizabethan-style ruffles, and red makeup on her eyes. Before performing, she used John Lennon's famous line that he said before the Beatles'

Lady Gaga meets the Queen of England in December 2009. Dressed in a red latex dress, Gaga shook the Queen's hand and then curtsied.

performed for the Queen in 1963: "Good evening, Blackpool. Let me hear you rattle your jewelry."

The Daily Mirror reported that Lady Gaga was planning to include a shocking suicide act in her performance, but she was advised that it would not be appropriate. Instead, her piano was elevated on stilts and she sat on a swing suspended 12 feet in the air. "I've had to tone things down generally, but it doesn't matter because I'm a massive fan of the Queen," says Lady Gaga. "I was so excited and have even been practicing my curtsy." According to *The Sun*, the Queen chuckled when the pop star curtsied for her and shook her hand.

Back home in the United States, Barbara Walters named Lady Gaga one of the 10 Most Fascinating People of 2009; her report aired on ABC on December 9, 2009. For their one-on-one interview, Lady Gaga chose a conservative black Chanel suit. "When I met her, she was quite a lady and not gaga at all," said Walters. Lady Gaga showed respect to Walters by removing her trademark sunglasses and saying, "You know I don't take my glasses off for many interviews, but I'll take them off for you." Walters told her that she was surprised to see such a serious and articulate woman. "You're not at all what I expected. You're much more," she said.

Lady Gaga knows when to tone down her legendary fashion statements for royalty, world leaders, and celebrity interviewers, but she also believes there is nothing wrong with her creative and often risqué outfits. She also believes that the nuns from New York's Convent of the Sacred Heart Catholic High School, where she attended school, would approve. "I haven't had any feedback from the nuns, but it's interesting because I think everyone assumes that because I went to such a religious school perhaps they don't appreciate what I'm doing now. But it is quite the opposite," Lady Gaga says. "I got a really solid education, in particular how to analyze art, how to make art. If anything, my teachers are sort of nodding their heads and saying, 'She did a good job of using her artistic abilities to really create a new kind of pop.' "

Shortly before the world knew her as Lady Gaga, Stefani Germanotta performed at music festivals like Lollapalooza in Chicago, Illinois. Back in those days, Gaga wasn't popular enough to entertain on the big stage. That all has changed now!

Growing Up Gaga

*L*ady Gaga, of Italian-American descent, was born Stefani Joanne Angelina Germanotta (jer-man-AH-tah) on March 28, 1986, in New York City. She was raised in a wealthy neighborhood on the city's Upper West Side. Her parents, Joseph and Cynthia Germanotta, called her Joanne. Joseph is an Internet entrepreneur, and Cynthia is a telecommunications assistant. Stefani has a younger sister, Natalie.

As a young girl, Stefani sang along with her miniature plastic tape recorder, which often played songs by Michael Jackson and Cyndi Lauper. When her parents took her out for dinner in fancy New York restaurants, she would dance around the table, using the breadsticks as batons. On the nights she stayed home, she would greet her baby-sitter in only her birthday suit! "I was always an entertainer. I was a ham as a little girl, and I'm a ham today," she says in her biography on ladygaga.com. Additionally, she had big dreams at a very early age. "I had this dream, and I really wanted to be a star. I was almost a monster in the way that I was fearless with my ambitions," she told Barbara Walters during a 2010 interview on ABC's *20/20*.

At age four, she learned how to play piano by ear. By the time she was thirteen, Stefani had written her first piano ballad. At fourteen, she was performing in New York clubs.

Unlike most other teenagers, Stefani was hitting the New York hotspots — with her mother. "I've been playing out in clubs since I was in high school," she said. "Since I was fifteen, my mum used to take me [because] I was too young to get in. My mum was super cool. She'd help me sign up and perform." During college, Stefani rode her bike or walked to different clubs in New York on the Lower East Side and in the

Lady Gaga traded in her crazy attire for a conservative look when she sang for President Barack Obama and a crowd at the Human Rights Campaign Dinner on October 10, 2009.

East Village. She knew that becoming a great success wouldn't come without a little bit of pain. "You've got to play clubs. You've got to do amazing [things]. You've got to fail. You've got to get standing ovations and need to be booed off the stage," she said in a March 2009 *FOXNews* article.

Performing in front of strangers at night was a great escape from the pain Stefani suffered during her days in school. She attended Convent of the Sacred Heart High School, a high-class New York private school, but she hated it. The unique fashion sense that has made her famous is the same one that her classmates teased her about daily. In August 2009, *Dailyfill.com* quoted her as saying, "I always gravitated to different things. I was eccentric. I went to a school full of spoiled kids. [They made fun of] the way I dressed and talked. Even when I went to art school I was a bit of a sore thumb, but that's because I wasn't interested in being put through the sausage machine. I could be insecure—all that 'who's saying what behind your back' stuff, but I hid in my work."

As a young girl, Stefani sang along with her miniature plastic tape recorder, which often played songs by Michael Jackson and Cyndi Lauper.

At seventeen, she was one of twenty people in the world to gain early admission to one of the world's most prestigious art schools, New York University's Tisch School of the Arts, to study music. Stefani wanted to pursue a music career, so at age nineteen, she dropped out of Tisch to start on the path of her dream. She told her parents she didn't need their money and moved to Clinton Street in New York, where she waited tables at the Comelia Street Café, performed at several local clubs, and tried to get noticed. Her biography on IMDb.com reports her as saying, "I made music and worked my way from the bottom up. I didn't know somebody who knew somebody, who knew somebody. If I have any advice for anybody, it's to just do it yourself, and don't waste time trying to get a favor." She didn't mind working hard to promote herself. "I would make demo tapes and send them around; then I would jump on my bike and pretend to be Lady Gaga's manager. I'd make $300 at work and spend it all on Xeroxes to make posters."

> "I made music and worked my way from the bottom up. . . . If I have any advice for anybody, it's to just do it yourself."

While Stefani was starting to become popular in nightclubs and gentlemen's clubs, her father wasn't so sure of his daughter's shocking—and revealing—stage presence. The first time he saw her perform, she was wearing something from her "shock art" collection: a leopard G-string. "It wasn't really so easy for my dad, especially in the beginning," she told Barbara Walters. "We didn't talk for months after the first time he saw me play, and my mother told me he was afraid I was, like, mentally unstable."

Stefani's dad supported her, though, especially during hard times. In 2005, Stefani was headed down a path lined with drugs, admitting she would lock herself in a room alone with cocaine, a mirror, and music by The Cure. Her father convinced her that she was messing up her life. Gaga admits she still likes to party, but she was quoted in an article on Coverawards.com in September 2009 saying that cocaine is "no longer a tool for my creativity."

CHAPTER 3

Familiar "Poker Face"

*I*n 2006, Stefani met up with Rob Fusari, a multiplatinum producer who had worked with Destiny's Child and Will Smith. Fusari's friend was watching Stefani perform at the Cutting Room, a New York nightclub, and recommended that she talk to Fusari. Over the next four months, she traveled to New Jersey seven days a week to work with him. Knowing how difficult it was for women to succeed in the rock genre, he asked her to ditch the rock sound and take a different path. According to an article in *The [New Jersey] Star-Ledger*, "Fusari said, 'Stef, what if we sit down today, abandon what we were going to work on and I'll sit at the drum machine, do a beat and we'll start with a more dance thing?' " By the end of the day, they had created "Beautiful, Dirty, Rich," a song that was eventually released on Gaga's debut album, *The Fame*, in 2008. Fusari took the song to Joshua Sarubin at Island Def Jam, who, according to *The Star-Ledger*, exclaimed, "I gotta get this girl in here next week!"

Sarubin recognized Stefani's talent right away. "She sat down at the piano in a showcase room and the way she played and the lyrics and the way she acted and sang was just so different and in your face, and you couldn't turn away," he said. "She was wearing these crazy white thigh-high boots and a black mini-dress and she had this presence like, 'I'm sexy and I don't care what anybody has to say about it.' "

Fusari takes some credit for the birth of the "Lady Gaga" stage name. "Every day, when Stef came to the studio, instead of saying hello, I would start singing [the '80s Queen tune] 'Radio Ga Ga.' That was her entrance song." Gaga adds that her name came from a love of the single "Radio Ga Ga" and her friends who watched her perform in New York. They told her she was theatrical and called her Gaga—another word for "crazy." The name stuck, and now the world knows her as nothing other than Lady Gaga. She told Oprah Winfrey, however, that she prefers just to be called "Gaga." "I don't like Lady. It feels so weird," she says.

". . . the way [Gaga] played and the lyrics and the way she acted was just so different and in your face."

At the age of nineteen, Gaga signed briefly with Def Jam Records in Los Angeles, but no recordings came from that partnership. Three months later, the label dropped her without explanation. Gaga was hurt and questioned if she should continue pursuing a music career. Instead of quitting, though, she became more determined to rebel through her appearance, and her outfits became crazier than ever. In 2007, Fusari helped her sign with Streamline Records, an imprint of Interscope Records. During this time, she teamed up with a glam-rock deejay named Lady Starlight. Together, they launched a comedy-burlesque show for Manhattan clubs. Fusari didn't approve of her using the music they worked so hard on to be used in this way, so they parted ways. "I miss her, but I'm also very proud of her and happy that it went as big as it did," he said.

During this time, Lady Gaga continued to pursue her own record deal, but was also asked to write songs for other artists, including Britney Spears, the Pussycat Dolls, New Kids on the Block, Fergie, and the Black-Eyed Peas. Singer-songwriter and record producer Akon was paying attention to her impressive talent and asked Interscope chairman Jimmie Iovine to sign her to a joint deal with Interscope and his own label, Kon Live Distribution, in 2008.

Paris Hilton and Lady Gaga hang out in the DJ booth at Maya London in January 2009. Maya is considered "the home of fashion; where styles are made and trends are set." Gaga, no doubt, fit right in!

"She was a star before the fame," Akon told Giuliana Rancic on the 2010 Grammy Red Carpet. "Instantly, from the moment I saw her, I said, that's a star." He says that her quick success is due to a strong work ethic, but Lady Gaga often gives credit for her success to the gay community, who has embraced her style and music. "She's brave. She's fresh. She's different. She's bold. You gotta take her as she is. That's the beauty of it. You're forced to like her the way she is without extra stuff added," he said.

> "She's brave. She's fresh. She's different. She's bold. You gotta take her as she is. That's the beauty of it," Akon said of Gaga.

Once on a roll with Kon Live, it didn't take long for an album to materialize. In August 2008, Gaga's debut album, *The Fame*, was released with great success. It went to number one in four countries and topped the Billboard Top Electronic Albums chart in the United States. Gaga is the first artist in the seventeen-year history of Billboard's Pop Songs chart to have four singles ("Poker Face," "Just Dance," "Love Game," and "Paparazzi") from a debut album go all the way to number one. "Poker Face" was also nominated for Best Dance Recording at the 51st Grammy Awards in 2009. By the end of that year, Gaga released her second studio album, *The Fame Monster*, which, launched her single "Bad Romance" almost immediately to the top of the charts. At the 52nd Grammy Awards in 2010, Gaga was nominated in six categories; she brought home awards for Best Dance Recording and Best Electronic/Dance Album.

Lady Gaga has opened in concert for popular musical acts like New Kids on the Block and the Pussycat Dolls, but in

Oversized shoulders — a favorite fashion for Gaga — are often featured in her one-of-a-kind wardrobe. She never misses an opportunity to add some glitz and sparkle.

2009, she embarked on her own with The Fame Ball Tour. Since she started touring, Gaga's stage routines have become more refined, but she still includes some of her favorite elements, such as disco balls, hot pants, sequins, and stiletttos. She incorporates that image into what she calls a "more fierce and more of a conceptual show with a vision for pop performance art." That thought is behind her records as well. On her website, she says, "I almost want to trick people into hanging with something that is really cool with a pop song. It's almost like the spoonful of sugar and I'm the medicine."

Many of Lady Gaga's stage outfits are glam-rock inspired—sparkly and bold. Her performances are just as bold and over the top.

CHAPTER 4

Gaga Ooh La La

*L*ady Gaga was influenced by musicians David Bowie, Freddie Mercury (lead singer of Queen), Madonna, and Michael Jackson. "I adored Freddie Mercury and Queen had a hit called 'Radio Ga Ga.' That's why I love the name," she says. "Freddie was unique—one of the biggest personalities in the whole of pop music." Lady Gaga was also intrigued by the idea of how rock, pop music, and theater could blend. "When I discovered Queen and David Bowie is when it really came together for me and I realized that I could do all three," she says in her biography. "I look at those artists as icons in art. It's not just about the music. It's about the performance, the attitude, the look. It's everything, and that is where I live as an artist and that is what I want to accomplish."

Lady Gaga's "artistry" comes out in her music as well as her attire. "I'm inspired by '70s glam, decadence, skyscrapers, Madonna," she told *People*. She also claims in her biography on her website that her fashion has been inspired by her rock-star girlfriends, Peggy Bundy, and the late Donatella Versace.

Gaga claims her creativity comes naturally. "I've always been a creative person. Something that people don't know about me is that I put a lot of thought into my performances,"

she told Oprah in January 2010. Every day, she wakes up, goes to the computer, and goes through all of her music files. "The hardest part of my job is that I'm bossy. I spend hours and hours calling everyone on my team to put together the show of my dreams," she adds. The softer side comes out minutes before she goes on stage. That's when Gaga and her group say a prayer together. They end the prayer by saying the name "Joanne," referring to Gaga's deceased aunt. "I believe she's on stage with us every night," she told Oprah's film crew during a backstage interview before a concert.

Gaga's creative wardrobe has received mixed reviews. Following the 2010 Grammy Awards, Adam Lambert appeared on *Entertainment Tonight* with his Best and Worst Dressed List. Lady Gaga appeared on neither list, but, instead, was given her own category. "I have created the 'Glambert Award' that goes to Lady Gaga. She lives on her own fashion planet. She looked like fashion on parade," he said.

In May 2009, Lady Gaga appeared on the cover of *Rolling Stone* wearing only pink bubbles. In an interview with *Rolling Stone's* Brian Hiatt, Lady Gaga admitted that she's different from other pop singers, saying, "I think I'm changing what people think is sexy."

Lady Gaga teamed up with Beyoncé in 2010 for the single "Telephone."
Speaking about the video, Gaga told Ryan Seacrest on this KIIS-FM radio
show in February 2010, "What I like about it is, it's a real true pop event.
When I was younger I was always excited there was a big giant event
happening in pop music and that's what I wanted this to be."

Not everyone agrees with that. Producer Rob Fusari was often reluctant to let Gaga go out in public in her outrageous outfits. He recalled one particular outfit she created to wear around Miami. "It looked like a one-piece bathing suit with these shoes that looked three feet tall and a ripped-up jean skirt with one leg attached. The jewelry looked like it was from Mars. I'm like, 'Stef, . . . I'm not walking next to you.'"

Joshua Sarubin recalls the same thing. "She would go to Starbucks and I would be embarrassed to go with her because of her outfits. She did it 24/7 and that to me is what makes a star. She lived it." Gaga defended her attire in a video

Lady Gaga walks the Red Carpet at the Grammys in January 2010. With sparkly moon boots and a space-age solar system dress, Gaga truly looked out of this world!

montage on *E!*'s *Countdown to the Grammys* on January 31, 2010: "I dress like this all the time. You're not going to catch me at the grocery store in flip-flops." She has stayed focused on making a fashion statement, keeping a scrapbook of ideas she would see in magazines—everything from clothes to neon signs to a hand with a ring—nothing is off limits for Gaga's creative mind. It makes sense that she was named one of *People* magazine's 2009 best fashion rebels.

Lady Gaga might be the queen of shock value with her eccentric attire, but she has the respect of many celebrities who see that beauty is deeper than what she wears. Whoopi Goldberg, who attended Queen Elizabeth's event in London with Lady Gaga, told *The View* audience on January 22, 2010, "She has it. She has that thing you want in a performer. She's magnificent. She's different and not like anybody else."

Barbara Walters agrees, and says that behind the bizarre attire is a woman who "is interesting. She is very vulnerable. The way she made herself different is by making herself outrageous." In an interview with Walters, Gaga was asked about the biggest misconception of being Lady Gaga. "That I am artificial and attention-seeking," she said. "But the truth is that every bit of me is devoted to love and art. I aspire to be a teacher to my young fans who feel just like I felt when I was younger. I felt just like a freak. I want to liberate them. I want to free them of their fears and [let them] feel they can create their own space in the world."

> "It's about the performance, the attitude, the look. It's everything, and that is where I live as an artist."

CHAPTER 5

There's More to Gaga

*O*ften criticized for being a bit over the top in the creativity category, Lady Gaga is thankful that one company recognizes her talent. On January 7, 2010, she announced that she will serve as creative director for a specialty line of products for Polaroid. The company, best known for its instant-film cameras, planned to roll out the first Gaga-themed products by the end of 2010. According to a Polaroid spokesperson, Lady Gaga will be developing "imaging products" that include both the company's signature instant-film cameras as well as digital devices. At the Polaroid booth at the 2010 Consumer Electronics Show (CES) in Las Vegas, Gaga told the press, "I'm definitely a Polaroid camera girl. I really believe in the lifestyle and injecting the things that I love into [this]. . . . For me, what I'm really excited about is bringing back the artistry and the nature of Polaroid. Lifestyle, music, art, fashion . . . I am so excited to extend myself behind the scenes as a designer, and to—as my father puts it—finally have a real job."

Lady Gaga's interest in combining sound with fashion also inspired her to develop and launch Lady Gaga Heartbeats, a performance in-ear headphone. Partnering with

Dr. Dre's Monster Beats earphones company, Gaga created a new design and integrated a sound quality that would add emotion to the music. Features of the product, as mentioned on the Monstercable website, are described in this way: "The better your music sounds, the more emotional it is. Heartbeats faithfully reproduce artists' vocals and the music behind them, so you can hear the heartfelt emotion your favorite singer wants to share with you."

While in Las Vegas on January 7, 2010, Gaga announced a new red version of her original Heartbeat performance headphones, with proceeds of the red Heartbeat going to Bono's HIV/AIDS charity RED. "There will be a red Heartbeat that will also be packaged with an acoustic version of 'Poker Face,' " she said. Speaking of her fans, she told the crowd, "We really appreciate you little monsters."

Lady Gaga and Beyoncé attended the 4th Annual Women In Music event in New York City, where the P.S. 22 Chorus sang a tribute to women's achievements.

Lady Gaga's interest goes beyond her music, and that was evident in October 2009, when she attended the National Equality March in Washington, D.C. During dinner the night before, she told the crowd: "You are inspiring a tremendous number of young people, and I know that tomorrow is going to be just as memorable as tonight was. And I promise to continue and to love and be loyal, to stand up for and to continue to challenge the world for all of you."

The next day, Lady Gaga attended the National Equality March, publicly urging an end to homophobia in the music industry. Lady Gaga was welcomed with open arms. She said that even with all of her international success, appearing in front of that accepting crowd on The Mall in Washington, D.C., was "the single most important moment of my career."

While Lady Gaga lives a busy life between making her own music and developing products, this pop star tries to find time to do the other thing she loves—cooking! She loves spending time in her kitchen and credits her Italian heritage for her cooking skills and love of food. "Secretly, I'm a wanna-be foodie," she told Oprah in January 2010. "The rumors I am a dab hand in the kitchen are completely true. I come from an Italian family—what more can I say? I love to cook. I am really good at Italian food. So I make great meatballs, pasta and all sorts."

But who is Lady Gaga—really?

When Akon was interviewed on the Red Carpet in 2010, he wore a black Lady Gaga T-shirt, honoring the woman he helped bring up in the music industry. He was asked about Lady Gaga's secretive side, but he disputed that she has one. "Believe it or not, she's not really secretive. She's wide open. That's why people love her so much. She's completely comfortable," he said.

She's giving, too. On January 24, 2010, every dollar from ticket and merchandise sales from The Monster Ball concert in New York went toward Haiti earthquake relief.

Gaga spoke to a crowd of more than 200,000 at the National Equality March in Washington, D.C., in October 2009. Passionate about gay rights, Gaga considered this event to be a highlight of her career.

Gaga is also very connected to her "monster" fans, and speaks candidly about how much they continue to give her a reason to write music. "I love my fans so much, and more than anything, I discovered lots of things about myself that I didn't know before through my fans," she told *MTV News*.

In an interview with Oprah, Gaga confessed that she doesn't have a lot of friends but that her "monsters" are where her friendships reside. Gaga said she really feels her fans' love during her performances. "I have a very raw performance style and [I'm] leaving my heart on the stage every night, and they were giving me so much back in return that when the show was over, I wanted to write," she explained. "I wanted to make music."

She is not shy about making sure her fans always know how much she appreciates them. Often, she uses Twitter to convey her thoughts to them. On January 31, 2010, Lady Gaga was at the Los Angeles Staples Center for the 52nd Annual Grammy Awards. Backstage before the show, she tweeted to her fans: "Backstage getting ready, feels like you're here with me tonight little monsters. Thank you for a beautiful year full of love and music. Iloveu. I am so grateful to all of you for your loyalty and love. I would never be here without u."

> **"I love my fans so much, and more than anything, I discovered lots of things about myself that I didn't know before through my fans."**

She is also never shy about encouraging her fans. During the Oprah interview, Gaga was asked what message she wants everyone to receive. "I want them to free themselves and be proud of who they are," she said. "Celebrate what you don't like about yourself. I perform every night and look into your beautiful eyes and I love you so much. I know how you feel. I never gave up on my dream. It's about what makes you feel good."

Lady Gaga didn't grow up in a famous family, rise to the top of charts with help of *American Idol*, or gain fame through the help of a reality show. Instead, she believes she became a star the way a person is supposed to. "I played every club in New York City, and I bombed in every club, and then killed it in every club. I found myself as an artist. I learned how to survive as an artist, get real, and how to fail and then figure out who I was as a singer and performer. And I worked hard," she says in her biography. "And, now, I'm just trying to change the world one sequin at a time."

1986	Stefani Joanne Angelina Germanotta is born on March 28.
2000	As a teenager, she starts performing in New York nightclubs.
2003	She is one of twenty people to gain early admission to one of the world's most prestigious art schools, New York University's Tisch School of the Arts.
2005	She signs with Island Def Jam Music Group.
2007	She signs with Streamline Records.
2008	Her debut album, *The Fame*, is released in August.
2009	She releases her second studio album, *The Fame Monster*, and announces The Monster Ball Tour. Her first headlining North American tour, The Fame Ball Tour, opens on March 12. On December 11, she sings "Speechless" for Queen Elizabeth II. She is named one of *People* magazine's best fashion rebels of the year.
2010	She becomes the creative director and inventor of specialty products for Polaroid. She wins her first two Grammy Awards.

DISCOGRAPHY

Albums
2009   *The Fame Monster*
2008   *The Fame*

Singles
2010   "Telephone"
2009   "Eh Eh (Nothing Else I Can Say)"
          "Love Game"
          "Paparazzi"
          "Bad Romance"
2008   "Just Dance"
          "Poker Face"

Tours
2010   The Monster Ball Tour
2009   The Fame Ball Tour

Books

Edwards, Posey. *Lady Gaga: Me and You*. London: Orion, 2010.

Parvis, Sarah. *Lady Gaga*. Kansas City, MO: Andrews McMeel Publishing, 2010.

Rafter, Dan, and Tess Fowler (illustrator). *Fame: Lady Gaga*. Vancouver, WA: Bluewater Productions, 2010.

Waters, Rosa. *Beyoncé*. Broomall, PA: Mason Crest Publishers, 2007.

Works Consulted

Frere-Jones, Sasha. "Ladies Wild." *The New Yorker*, April 27, 2009. http://www.newyorker.com/arts/critics/musical/2009/04/27/090427crmu_music_frerejones

Grigoriadis, Vanessa. "125 Minutes With Lady Gaga." *New York Magazine*, March 29, 2009. http://nymag.com/news/intelligencer/encounter/55653/

Interview with Barbara Walters on ABC's *20/20*, January 22, 2010.

Kaufman, Gil. "Lady Gaga Hooks Up with Polaroid for 'Specialty Products.' " *MTV.com*, January 7, 2010. http://www.mtv.com/news/articles/1629203/20100107/lady_gaga.jhtml

———."President Obama 'Opens' for Lady Gaga at Human Rights Campaign Dinner." *MTV.com*, October 12, 2009. http://www.mtv.com/news/articles/1623591/20091012/lady_gaga.jhtml

"Lady Gaga: Addicted to Cocaine?" *Coverawards.com*, August 8, 2009. http://coverawards.com/2009/09/08/lady-gaga-addicted-to-cocaine/

"Lady Gaga at HRC Dinner." *Huffingtonpost.com*, November 11, 2009. http://www.huffingtonpost.com/2009/10/11/lady-gaga-at-hrc-dinner-p_n_316572.html

"Lady Gaga Loves to Cook." *Contactmusic.com*, January 8, 2010. http://www.contactmusic.com/news.nsf/story/lady-gaga-loves-to-cook_1127996

"Lady GaGa Praises Her Catholic Education." *Monstersandcritics.com*, May 30, 2009. http://www.monstersandcritics.com/people/news/article_1480353.php/Lady_GaGa_praises_her_Catholic_education

"Lady GaGa: Press Conference in Israel." *Dailyfill.com*, August 16, 2009. http://www.dailyfill.com/Lady-GaGa-Press-Conference-in-Israel-32621/

Lawler, Danielle. "Lady GaGa Meets the Queen at Royal Variety Performance." *Daily Mirror*, December 8, 2009. http://www.mirror.co.uk/celebs/news/2009/12/08/mad-meets-maj-115875-21881111/

Live E! on the Red Carpet, January 31, 2010.

McKay, Hollie. "Lady Gaga: I Have Been Clubbing Since Childhood." *FOXnews.com*, March 4, 2009. http://www.foxnews.com/entertainment/2009/03/04/lady-gaga-clubbing-childhood/

Rose, Lisa. "Lady Gaga's Outrageous Persona Born in Parsippany, New Jersey." *The Star-Ledger*, January 21, 2010. http://www.nj.com/entertainment/music/index.ssf/2010/01/lady_gaga_her_outrageous_perso.html

On the Internet

Gaga Daily
www.gagadaily.com

Lady Gaga Online
www.ladygagaonline.net

Official Web Site
www.ladygaga.com